DISNEY · PIXAR

FINDING NEMO

Bruce's Bonzer Joke Book

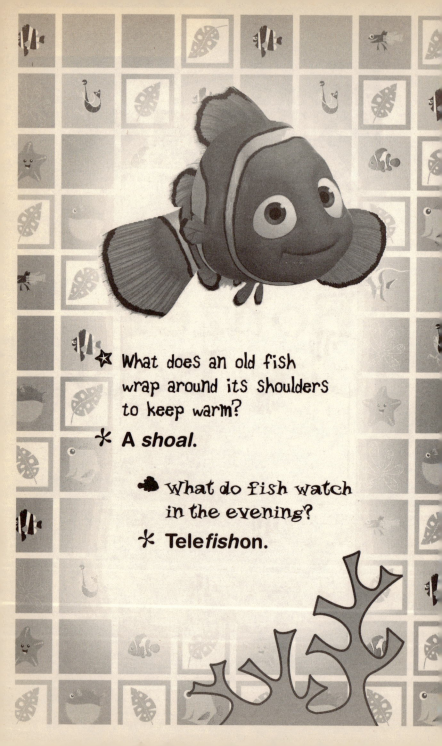

☆ What does an old fish wrap around its shoulders to keep warm?

✱ A *shoal*.

What do fish watch in the evening?

✱ Tele*fish*on.

Disney · PIXAR
FINDING NEMO

Bruce's Bonzer Joke Book

Crush: 'Knock, knock.'

Squirt: 'Who's there?'

Crush: 'Toot.'

Squirt: 'Toot who?'

Crush: '*Toot* turtle doves
and a partridge
in a pear tree.'

PUFFIN BOOKS

Published by the Penguin Group
Penguin Books Ltd, 80 Strand, London WC2R 0RL, England
Penguin Putnam Inc., 375 Hudson Street, New York, New York 10014, USA
Penguin Books Australia Ltd, 250 Camberwell Road, Camberwell,
Victoria 3124, Australia
Penguin Books Canada Ltd, 10 Alcorn Avenue, Toronto, Ontario,
Canada M4V 3B2
Penguin Books India (P) Ltd, 11 Community Centre, Panchsheel Park,
New Delhi – 110 017, India
Penguin Books (NZ) Ltd, Cnr Rosedale and Airborne Roads, Albany, Auckland,
New Zealand
Penguin Books (South Africa) (Pty) Ltd, 24 Sturdee Avenue,
Rosebank 2196, South Africa

Penguin Books Ltd, Registered Offices: 80 Strand,
London WC2R 0RL, England

www.penguin.com

Published in Puffin Books 2003
1

Design by Dan Newman/Perfect Bound
Written by Kay Barnham

Set in JorgeNormal, Chuck Bold and Helvetica Sans Rounded

Made and printed in England by Clays Ltd, St Ives plc

British Library Cataloguing in Publication Data
A CIP catalogue record for this book is available from the British Library

ISBN 0–141–31660–8

What happens to sleepy fish at the edge of the reef?

* They *Drop-off.*

Which sea creatures come calling at Christmas?

* *Coral* singers.

What is the best way to communicate with a fish?

Drop it a line!

Why is a fish easy to weigh?

It has its own scales.

Which fish can perform operations?

A *sturgeon*.

What do you call
a fish with no eyes?

Fsh.

What do you call a fish
with three eyes?

Fiiish!

Why didn't the sailor's
radio work when the sea
was rough?

It was on the wrong
wavelength.

☆ Why are goldfish orange?

✳ **The water makes them rusty.**

🐟 Which fish love it when the sea freezes over?

✳ **Skates.**

Which fish has a halo and wings?

* An angelfish.

What's the difference between a fish and a piano?

* You can't *tuna* fish!

What game do fish like playing most?

* **Name that *tuna*.**

Where do tinned fish go on holiday?

* **To *Sardine*ia.**

✫ Why was Old King Cole
   like a happy fish?

✳ Because he was
   a merry old *sole*.

🐟 What do you call someone
   who scoops up lots of
   fish in one go?

✳ Annette.

Why did the plaice go to the doctor?

* Because he was feeling a bit flat.

☆ Where do little fish go every morning?

* To *plaice* school.

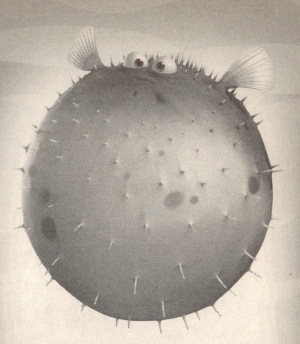

🐡 How do sea creatures carry big things?

✳ In a *whale*barrow.

🐠 What is full of holes yet can still hold water?

✳ A sea-sponge.

☆ What fish is the most valuable?

✳ A goldfish.

🐟 Where do jellyfish sleep on a campsite?

✳ In *tentacles*.

Where do fish put their rubbish?

In a *whaleie* bin.

What fish sits on a plate and wobbles?

A jellyfish.

Which games do fish play?

Tide-and-seek and
bass the parcel.

What did the hake say
to his naughty son?

'For goodness *hake*!'

✭ What is Squirt's favourite
playground ride?

✷ The *seashore*.

 Where does seaweed
look for a job?

✷ In the '*kelp* wanted'
adverts.

Did you hear about the athletic fish who swam round and round the island?

* He lapped the shore.

☆ What does an Australian fish call a fishy friend?

* Mate.

What does an Australian
fish with a cold call a
fishy friend?

✳ Bait.

Which seabird can dance?

✳ A pelican can.

☆ Why are seabirds easy to fool?

✳ Because they're *gull*ible.

🐟 What do you call a bird that floats on the sea's surface?

✳ Bob.

Who is the cleverest seabird?

* Albert Ross.

What kind of tank isn't filled with soldiers?

* A fish tank.

Which fish hangs in the sky
and shines at night?

* A moonfish.

Which fish does
a pirate carry?

* A swordfish.

☆ Where do fish go to complete their education?

✳ *Finishing school.*

🐟 What do fish like to chew?

✳ **Bubblegum.**

🐟 What fish lives in the jungle?

✳ **A tiger shark.**

✿ **'Knock, knock.'**
✳ *'Who's there?'*
✿ **'Ann.'**
✳ *'Ann who?'*
✿ **'Annchovy.'**

🐠 How do you rate Nemo's good looks, from one to ten?

✳ **He's off the scale!**

What's the world's laziest fish?

The kipper.

What happens when fish don't clean the bath out?

They leave a tide mark.

What is Bruce's favourite sort of meal?

A quick bite.

'Knock, knock.'

'Who's there?'

'A Fred.'

'A Fred who?'

'Who's *a Fred* of sharks?!'

☆ What do you call
Anchor when he's
playing poker?

✳ **A card shark.**

🐟 What sweet, crunchy
snacks do you find
at the bottom of the sea?

✳ *Abysscuits.*

🐟 What did the fisherman
push around the
supermarket?

✳ **A shopping *trawler.***

🐟 Where do divers
go on holiday?

✳ sCuba.

🐟 What do Bruce, Anchor
and Chum sing at
Christmas?

✳ 'Shark the herald
angels sing'

Why does Nemo like arcade games?

He's a *finball* wizard.

What do you say to a scary anglerfish?

'Glow away!'

What do you get from a bad-tempered shark?

* As far away as possible.

Why does Anchor like head-banging at pop concerts?

* He's a hammerhead shark.

What instrument can
Bruce play with his teeth?

The **sharp**.

What does a shark's
dinner taste like?

Brill.

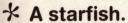 What does Chum
paint on his face
before he goes out?

✻ **Makop.**

 Which fish has a
twinkle in its eye?

✻ **A starfish.**

What is Bernie and Baz the crabs, favourite fruit?

✱ **The crab apple.**

Why are dolphins cleverer than humans?

✱ **They can train a human to stand at the side of the pool and feed them fish.**

Which sea creature rides a horse and thinks he's an outlaw?

* Billy the Squid.

Why are fishing boots really warm?

* Because they have *electric 'eels.*

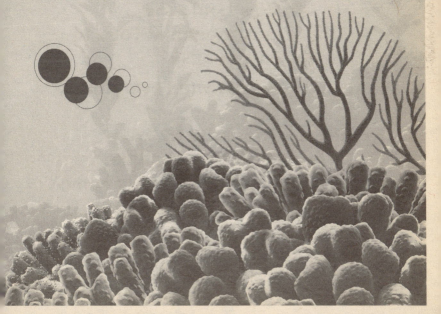

Who held the baby
octopus for ransom?

* *Squid*nappers.

How do little squids
go to school?

* By octo*bus*.

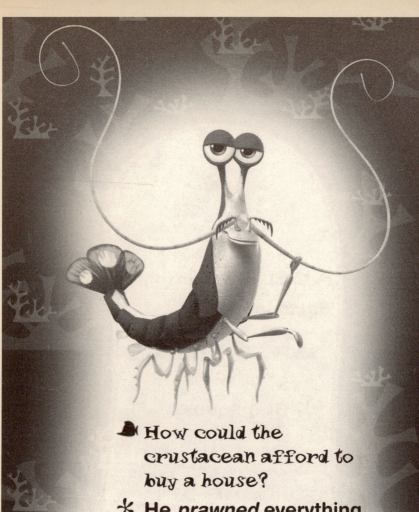

How could the crustacean afford to buy a house?

* He *prawned* everything.

Bernie: 'What did the sea creature say when the hermit crab stole his home?'

Baz: 'Don't be so *shell*fish!'

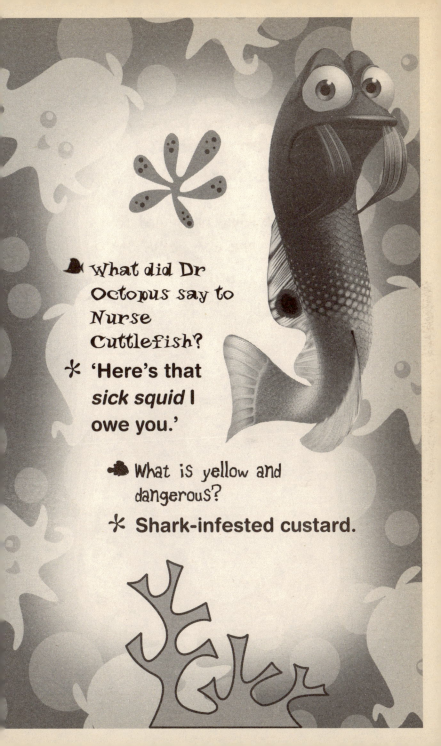

What did Dr Octopus say to Nurse Cuttlefish?

* 'Here's that *sick squid* I owe you.'

What is yellow and dangerous?

* Shark-infested custard.

What item of clothing does Crush wear when it's cold?

*A *turtleneck*.

What happened to the cold jellyfish?

*It set.

What was the caviar's
favourite hobby?

* It liked to *roe*
a boat.

How do you get two
whales in a Mini?

* Down the M4
motorway.

What's a whale's favourite game?

* *Swallow* the leader.

What's the saddest creature in the sea?

* The blue whale.

'Knock, knock.'

'Who's there?'

'Whale.'

'Whale who?'

'Whaleway twain.'

Which sea creatures cry the most?

Whales.

What do you call a whale who likes text messaging?

Moby.

What do you call a whale who likes to look up words?

*Moby Dick*tionary.

What do you get if you cross a shark with a parrot?

An animal that talks your head off!

What did the underwater cop say about the barracuda's dodgy deal?

* 'That smells fishy.'

Did you hear the one about the fish that gambled and lost?

* He had his chips.

How are fish 'n' chip shops nasty to fish?

* They batter them.

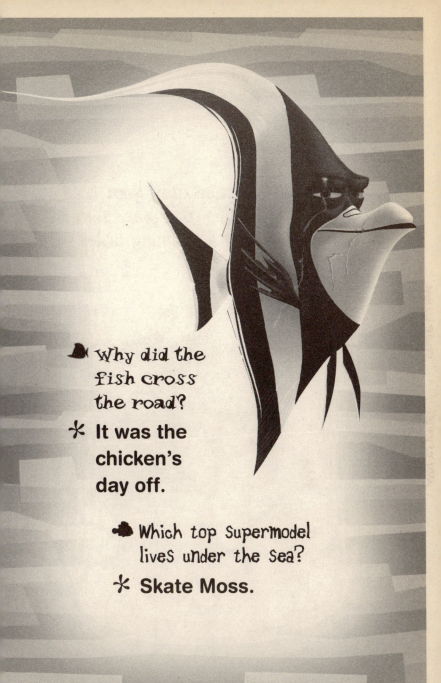

Why did the
fish cross
the road?

It was the
chicken's
day off.

Which top Supermodel
lives under the sea?

Skate Moss.

How does the sea
say goodbye?

* With a wave.

Which underwater game is
played with two cues, sixteen
balls and a spinning table?

* Whirlpool.

🐟 What is the eel's
favourite dance?

✳ **The** *conger*.

🐟 What did the photographer
use to take underwater
pictures?

✳ **A fish-eye lens.**

Did you hear the one about the fisherman who fell in love with the beautiful fish?

* She was a good catch.

What do you call a turtle with a seagull on his head?

* Cliff!

Why is the back of a fish like the last page of a storybook?

* They're both the end of a tail.

What lies at the bottom of the sea and shakes?

* A nervous wreck.

🐟 Why was the sand wet?

✳ **Because the sea weed!**

🐟 What do you call a shy
fish who likes to fool
his fishy friends?

✳ **A red herring.**

Where do you find a crab with no legs?

Exactly where you left it!

What does a scuba diver wear to an underwater wedding?

A wetsuit.

Where do birds cross the sea?

At the pelican crossing.

Why did the fish take hours to make a decision?

He wanted to *mullet* over.

What was the shellfish's favourite nursery rhyme?

* 'Winkle, winkle, little star'

What did the tuna call the submarine?

* A can of people!

How do you get rid of
a seal's creases?

With a *sealion*.

What's a dentist's
favourite subject
at college?

***Flossophy*.**

What happens when
dentists remove braces?

**Their trousers
fall down.**

What do you call someone who sits in a waiting room for hours and hours?

* Patient.

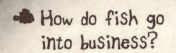 How do fish go into business?

* They start on a small scale!

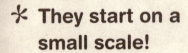 Did you hear about the royal tooth?

* It was crowned.

 What part of a fish
weighs the most?

❋ **Its scales!**

If fish lived on land,
what country would
they live in?

❋ *Finland.*

What part of a sandwich does a dentist like best?

The filling.

Where do dentists sail their boats?

Up root canals.

What does a royal dentist wear on his head?

A crown.

🐠 'Knock, knock.'

✳ 'Who's there?'

🐠 'Cod.'

✳ 'Cod who?'

🐠 '*Cod* you red-handed!'

🐠 What do dentists wear on their feet?

✳ **Espadrilles.**

Why couldn't Marlin afford a house?

Cos he didn't have *anemone*!

Did you hear about the tennis match between Bloat and Jacques?

Bloat won on points!

🐡 What happens to Bloat when he gets cross?

✳ **He blows up.**

🐟 Where does the Tank Gang like to play football?

✳ **On a football *Peach*.**

🐡 Why doesn't Deb enjoy Christmas?

✳ **She's a humbug.**

Where do the Tank Gang go to the movies?

* At the *dive*-in.

What happens to Deb when she can't see Peach?

* She's *Peachless*.

Did you hear about
the seafood diet?

* You *seafood* and eat it!

What did the mummy
fish say when she put
her baby to sleep?

* 'Sweet *breams*.'

What's Crush's
favourite drink?

* Squash.

What's in the middle of a jellyfish?

* A *jelly*button!

Why did Crush float on his back?

* He turned turtle.

What do you call a dried fruit from Sydney?

* An East Australian *Current*.